JUN 09

Values

Respect

Kimberley Jane Pryor

Marshall Cavendish
Benchmark

New York

This edition first published in 2009 in the United States of America by Marshall Cavendish Benchmark.

Marshall Cavendish Benchmark
99 White Plains Road
Tarrytown, NY 10591
www.marshallcavendish.us

First published in 2008 by
MACMILLAN EDUCATION AUSTRALIA PTY LTD
15–19 Claremont St, South Yarra 3141

Visit our Web site at www.macmillan.com.au or go directly to www.macmillanlibrary.com.au

Associated companies and representatives throughout the world.

Library of Congress Cataloging-in-Publication Data

Pryor, Kimberley Jane.
    Respect / by Kimberley Jane Pryor.
        p. cm. — (Values)
    Includes index.
    ISBN 978-0-7614-3128-2
    1. Respect—Juvenile literature. 2. Children—Conduct of life—Juvenile literature. I. Title.
    BJ1533.R4P79 2008
179'.9—dc22

                                                    2008001669

Edited by Helena Newton
Text and cover design by Christine Deering
Page layout by Raul Diche and Domenic Lauricella
Photo research by Naomi Parker and Legend Images

Printed in the United States

Acknowledgments
The author and the publisher are grateful to the following for permission to reproduce copyright material:

Front cover photograph of students listening to the teacher © bonnie jacobs/iStockphoto.com

Photos courtesy of:
© Richard Thomas/123RF, **13**; AAP Image/PhotoAlto, **5**; BananaStock, **6**; BrandX Pictures, **27**; Blend Images/Getty Images, **19**; Photodisc/Getty Images, **7, 15**; Image Source, **11, 16**; © Marcin Balcerzak/iStockphoto.com, **30**; © Martínez Banús/iStockphoto.com, **29**; © Galina Barskaya/iStockphoto.com, **21** © Franky De Meyer/iStockphoto.com, **17**; © geotrac/iStockphoto.com, **24**; © bonnie jacobs/iStockphoto.com, **1, 8**; © Elena Kouptsova-Vasic/iStockphoto.com, **3, 28**; © Mikhail Lavrenov/iStockphoto.com, **23**; © Cyril Le Roux/iStockphoto.com, **9**; © Sean Locke/iStockphoto.com, **20**; © Gloria-Leigh Logan/iStockphoto.com, **12**; © Andrew Manley/iStockphoto.com **14**; © Bradley Mason/iStockphoto.com, **25**; © Cliff Parnell/iStockphoto.com, **26**; © Lawrence Sawyer/iStockphoto.com, **22**; © Marzanna Syncerz/iStockphoto.com, **4**; Photos.com, **10, 18**.

While every care has been taken to trace and acknowledge copyright, the publisher tenders their apologies for any accidental infringement where copyright has proved untraceable. Where the attempt has been unsuccessful, the publisher welcomes information that would redress the situation.

For Nick, Ashley and Thomas

1 3 5 6 4 2

Contents

Glossary words

When a word is printed in **bold**, you can look up its meaning in the Glossary on page 31.

Values

Values are the things you believe in. They guide the way:

- you think

- you speak

- you **behave**

Values help you to play fairly with your friends in a sandpit.

Values help you to decide what is right and what is wrong. They also help you to live your life in a **meaningful** way.

Values help you to follow the rules when you play marbles with your friends.

Respect

Respect is treating others the way you would like to be treated. Speaking **politely** to people and being fair are ways to show respect.

It is fair to give everyone at a party a plate of party food and a drink.

Respect is also the feeling you have for someone you **admire**. It is the feeling you have for something or someone you think is important and special.

Clapping when someone has given a speech shows respect.

Respectful People

Respectful people listen when others are speaking. They wait for a turn to speak and do not interrupt others.

Listening to your teacher when she is speaking shows respect.

Respectful people care about other people's feelings and needs. They are **thoughtful** toward their family, friends, and neighbors.

This boy's friends understand that he is happy to be alone sometimes.

Showing Respect for Family

Family members show respect by giving each other **privacy**. They knock before they open a closed door.

This girl's family leaves her alone to read privately.

Respectful people take care of their homes and help to keep them clean and tidy. They do not jump on and off the furniture.

You show respect for your home when you keep the table neat and tidy.

Showing Respect for Friends

Friends show respect by being kind to each other. They do not make fun of each other or call each other names.

Friends show respect by treating each other well.

Respectful people ask before they **borrow** things from friends. They also take good care of things that they borrow from other people.

If you borrow a friend's skateboard, use it carefully so it does not get damaged.

Showing Respect for Neighbors

Neighbors show respect for each other by being **considerate**. It is considerate to call before visiting your neighbor.

It is considerate to call before visiting your neighbor.

14

Respectful people take pride in their neighborhood. They do not take or damage things that do not belong to them.

Respectful people do not pick flowers that are growing in their neighborhood.

Ways To Show Respect

There are many different ways to show respect for your family, friends, and neighbors. Being polite is a good way to start showing respect.

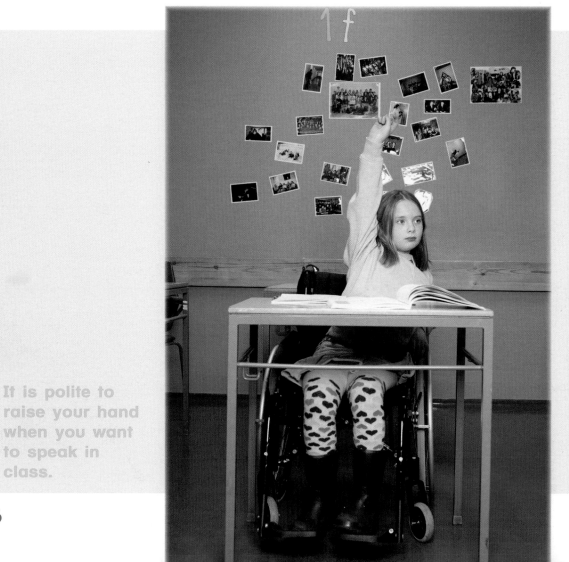

It is polite to raise your hand when you want to speak in class.

Taking care of other people's **property** shows respect. Thinking about the **rights** of others is another way to show respect. Accepting differences is also respectful.

People show respect for the rights of others by being quiet at the movies.

Being Polite

Being polite is a way to be respectful. It is polite to say "hello" to someone you know. It is also polite to say "please" and "thank you."

It is polite to say "thank you" when someone gives you a popsicle.

Polite people use good manners when they are with other people. They are pleasant to people they meet.

Smiling when you meet someone new is polite.

Being Considerate

Being considerate is another way to respect others. Considerate people are aware of other people's feelings.

Arriving on time for an appointment with the doctor is considerate.

Considerate people show respect for the rights of others. They try to make things easier for other people.

It is considerate to ride slowly on a shared bicycle and walking track.

Respecting Older People

Older people deserve respect because they have lived for a long time. They have **knowledge** and **skills** that younger people do not have yet.

An older family member may be able to teach you to fish.

You can show respect for older people by listening to their **opinions**. Holding doors open for older people shows respect. You can also offer them a seat on a bus.

Making sure an older person is comfortable is respectful.

Respecting Property

Respectful people take care of the property they share with others. They are careful with school property and playground equipment.

Carefully carrying sporting equipment shows respect.

Respectful people protect natural places by putting garbage in a can or taking it home. They also leave plants, animals, and natural objects where they found them.

Leaving shells at the beach is one way to protect natural places.

Accepting differences is another way to show respect. Respectful people treat all people with **dignity**.

These friends respect each other.

Accepting differences helps us to live peacefully with other people. It helps us to learn from others and to **cooperate** with others.

People from different backgrounds can have a lot of fun together.

27

Respecting Other Points of View

Respectful people try to understand other points of view, even if they disagree with them. Everyone has a different point of view.

Everyone deserves the chance to explain his or her point of view.

Each person sees the world in a different way. What matters to one person may not matter to another person.

Taking her stuffed toy to bed matters to this girl.

Personal Set of Values

There are many different values. Everyone has a personal set of values. This set of values guides people in big and little ways in their daily lives.

It is important for someone who gives advice to patients to show respect.

Glossary

admire	look up to
behave	act in a certain way
borrow	take something for a short time and agree to give it back
considerate	look out for other people's needs and feelings
cooperate	work together
dignity	treat people respectfully
knowledge	things you know and understand
meaningful	important or valuable
opinions	things you think
politely	acting with good manners
privacy	time alone away from others
property	something belonging to someone
rights	things that everyone should be allowed to do or have, such as the right to state or act on one's beliefs
skills	abilities that help you to do activities or jobs well
thoughtful	showing that you think and care about others

Index